Y0-CDD-040

The Little Tale of Peter Rabbit

The Little Tale of Peter Rabbit

by Beatrix Potter

A Coloring Book

Rendered for Coloring by
Anna Pomaska

Dover Publications, Inc., New York

Published in Canada by General Publishing Company, Ltd., 30 Lesmill Road, Don Mills, Toronto, Ontario.

Published in the United Kingdom by Constable and Company, Ltd., 3 The Lanchesters, 162–164 Fulham Palace Road, London W6 9ER.

The Little Tale of Peter Rabbit: A Coloring Book is a new work, first published by Dover Publications, Inc., in 1986. The text is reprinted unabridged from *The Tale of Peter Rabbit* by Beatrix Potter as first published in 1902. The illustrations, line renderings after Miss Potter's watercolors, were prepared specially for the present edition by Anna Pomaska.

International Standard Book Number: 0-486-25160-8

Manufactured in the United States of America
Dover Publications, Inc., 31 East 2nd Street,
Mineola, N.Y. 11501

Publisher's Note

Peter Rabbit is a naughty little bunny who is always getting into mischief. One morning, even though he knows he shouldn't, Peter decides to pay a visit to Mr. McGregor's garden. He sneaks in under the fence and feasts on the tasty vegetables he finds in the garden, but then his troubles begin.

Follow Peter's adventures in this classic Beatrix Potter tale, and while you enjoy reading about Peter's terrifying visit to Mr. McGregor's garden—including his near capture and his exciting escape to safety—you can have fun coloring the 27 charming pictures in this book.

Every word of *The Tale of Peter Rabbit* and every one of the famous Potter illustrations—adapted for your coloring enjoyment by noted children's book illustrator Anna Pomaska—is here. You'll delight in coloring the wonderful drawings of Peter, his family, Mr. McGregor and all the little animals Peter meets in the garden.

The Little Tale of Peter Rabbit

ONCE upon a time there were four little Rabbits, and their names were—

Flopsy,
Mopsy,
Cotton-tail,
and Peter.

They lived with their Mother in a sand-bank, underneath the root of a very big fir-tree.

'NOW, my dears,' said old Mrs. Rabbit one morning, 'you may go into the fields or down the lane, but don't go into Mr. McGregor's garden : your Father had an accident there ; he was put in a pie by Mrs. McGregor.'

'NOW run along, and don't get into mischief. I am going out.'

THEN old Mrs. Rabbit took a basket and her umbrella, and went through the wood to the baker's. She bought a loaf of brown bread and five currant buns.

FLOPSY, Mopsy, and Cotton-
tail, who were good little
bunnies, went down the lane
to gather blackberries;

BUT Peter, who was very naughty, ran straight away to Mr. McGregor's garden, and squeezed under the gate!

FIRST he ate some lettuces
and some French beans;
and then he ate some radishes;

AND then, feeling rather sick, he went to look for some parsley.

BUT round the end of a cucumber frame, whom should he meet but Mr. Mc-Gregor!

MR. McGREGOR was on his hands and knees planting out young cabbages, but he jumped up and ran after Peter, waving a rake and calling out, 'Stop thief!'

PETER was most dreadfully frightened; he rushed all over the garden, for he had forgotten the way back to the gate.

He lost one of his shoes among the cabbages, and the other shoe amongst the potatoes.

AFTER losing them, he ran on four legs and went faster, so that I think he might have got away altogether if he had not unfortunately run into a gooseberry net, and got caught by the large buttons on his jacket. It was a blue jacket with brass buttons, quite new.

PETER gave himself up for lost, and shed big tears; but his sobs were overheard by some friendly sparrows, who flew to him in great excitement, and implored him to exert himself.

MR. McGREGOR came up with a sieve, which he intended to pop upon the top of Peter; but Peter wriggled out just in time, leaving his jacket behind him,

AND rushed into the tool-shed, and jumped into a can. It would have been a beautiful thing to hide in, if it had not had so much water in it.

MR. McGREGOR was quite sure that Peter was somewhere in the tool-shed, perhaps hidden underneath a flower-pot. He began to turn them over carefully, looking under each.

Presently Peter sneezed— 'Kertyschoo!' Mr. McGregor was after him in no time,

AND tried to put his foot upon Peter, who jumped out of a window, upsetting three plants. The window was too small for Mr. McGregor, and he was tired of running after Peter. He went back to his work.

PETER sat down to rest; he was out of breath and trembling with fright, and he had not the least idea which way to go. Also he was very damp with sitting in that can.

After a time he began to wander about, going lippity—lippity—not very fast, and looking all round.

H E found a door in a wall; but it was locked, and there was no room for a fat little rabbit to squeeze underneath.

An old mouse was running in and out over the stone doorstep, carrying peas and beans to her family in the wood. Peter asked her the way to the gate, but she had such a large pea in her mouth that she could not answer. She only shook her head at him. Peter began to cry.

THEN he tried to find his way straight across the garden, but he became more and more puzzled. Presently, he came to a pond where Mr. McGregor filled his water-cans. A white cat was staring at some gold-fish; she sat very, very still, but now and then the tip of her tail twitched as if it were alive. Peter thought it best to go away without speaking to her; he had heard about cats from his cousin, little Benjamin Bunny.

H E went back towards the
tool-shed, but suddenly,
quite close to him, he heard
the noise of a hoe—scr-r-ritch,
scratch, scratch, scritch. Peter
scuttered underneath the
bushes. But presently, as
nothing happened, he came
out, and climbed upon a wheel-
barrow, and peeped over. The
first thing he saw was Mr.
McGregor hoeing onions. His
back was turned towards
Peter, and beyond him was
the gate!

PETER got down very
quietly off the wheel-
barrow, and started running
as fast as he could go, along
a straight walk behind some
black-currant bushes.

Mr. McGregor caught sight
of him at the corner, but Peter
did not care. He slipped underneath the gate, and was safe at
last in the wood outside the
garden.

M R. McGREGOR hung up
the little jacket and the
shoes for a scare-crow to
frighten the blackbirds.

PETER never stopped running or looked behind him till he got home to the big fir-tree.

He was so tired that he flopped down upon the nice soft sand on the floor of the rabbit-hole, and shut his eyes. His mother was busy cooking; she wondered what he had done with his clothes. It was the second little jacket and pair of shoes that Peter had lost in a fortnight!

I AM sorry to say that Peter was not very well during the evening.

His mother put him to bed, and made some camomile tea; and she gave a dose of it to Peter!

'One table-spoonful to be taken at bed-time.'

BUT Flopsy, Mopsy, and Cotton-tail had bread and milk and blackberries, for supper.

THE END.